Mikelnguut Yuarutait Yugcetun
Yup'ik Children's Songs

Mikelnguut Yuarutait Yugcetun
Yup'ik Children's Songs

Alaska Native Language Center
2006

Mikelnguut Yuarutait Yugcetun
Yup'ik Children's Songs

© 2006 Alaska Native Language Center
Fairbanks, Alaska

Printed in the United States of America
ISBN 1-55500-088-6

First printing 2006, 500 copies

Library of Congress Cataloging-in-Publication Data
Mikelnguut yuarutait yugcetun = Yup'ik children's songs
    p. cm.
  In Yup'ik with English translation.
  Principally with indications of the tunes.
  Includes indexes.
  ISBN 1-55500-088-6 (alk. paper)
    1. Children's songs, Yup'ik--Alaska--Texts. I. Alaska Native Language
Center. II. Title: Yup'ik children's songs.

ML54.6.M474 2006
782.42162'971400268--dc22   2006045963

Cover illustration by Moses Chanar. Other illustrations by
Moses Chanar, Paschal Afcan, Diane Dart, Teri Sloat, Marcia
Thompson, Richard Cook, Catherine Collier, Jeri Rudolph,
Al Foss.

Contents

Apertuutet
Kumaggaq

1977-aam uksuarani niiteqarraallruunga elitnauryaramek mikelngurnun Yugtun Imangami. Qaqiutnerrarlua high school-amnek maaten piunga ak'a imumi angliqarraallemni elitnauristemta Yugtun qalarcesqessuiterraarluta ciin waniwa qaneryuumaricesta?

Calingqarraallemni, canek elitnaurinermek-llu nallullruama, wangkun pikilii, "Qaillun-mi elitnauriqatarcia piqaqsaileng'erma?" Ak'anivkenii taũgaam elitua allani nunani wangtun ayuqellriartauciit—Yugtun qaneryugngaluteng kass'atun-llu, taugaam elitnaurissuutekameggnek akluinateng. Taum kinguani ayagayaurrlua Mamterillermun allanek ilamnek aipirlua elitnauristeńgurqaalrianek wangtun. Igaryaramek, elitnauryaranek, canek-llu allanek elitnaurat elitarkait kayungcaitnek. Tua-i tamamta piqainaurtengluta.

Yugtun elitnaurat caliviat ayagniqarraalleq 1970-ni ak'a qaqiucillrulliniameng kalikanek aturkaitnek elitnaurvigni mikelnguut qanemcikaitnek. Kass'artaungraata-llu tua-i ilait quyakluki aturluki—*Caũrluq, Kul'tilakessa'aq Pingayun-llu Taqukat.* Allanek cali ilangqerrsaaqut, ukuk tua-i kenkek'ngait mikelnguut. Makut kalikat quyaksaaqluki mumigtat yuarutet nutaan assikenrullruanka. Elitnaurinermek ayagniqarraallemni qavcirraullruut yuarutet elitnauriaqama atulallrenka.

Ukut pingayun—Iitaruaq, Aangaarraaq, Nuqaq'aq-llu—caliaqeqarraallruit makut yuarutet Yugtun mumigtat wall' ellmeggnek pilillrat atulalput elitnaurvimteńi. Calingerraallemni calillgutkellruanka ukut; taumek tua-i quyapialartua. Waniw' cali erinakek Iitaruankuk Aangaarraam-llu niitelaragka aturpalriik "Tang waniwa wiinga, nutaan itertua. . . " una-ll' cali "Kiarallruucircia wiinga. . . " Ukuk ilait-ll' allat yuarutet elitellrenka ilungulluki tua-i aturnauranka

elitevkangnaqluki elitnauranka. Aturaqamta tua-i elitnauranka
ilukegciluteng aturnaurtut.

Iitaruam, Aangaarraam, Nuqaqa'am-llu pinritevkenateng
ikaspallruitkut wangkutni elitnauristeńgurteqarraani, man'a
yuarun elitnauramta ircaquitnun temaitnun-llu ekluku. Quyam
tut'elaqiinga maa-irpak elitnaurvignun itraqama niitaqama
elitnaurayagarnek ilungluteng aturpalrianek Yugtun ukut
elitnauristeqarraaput yuarutiitnek atuagaqata.

Ukut waniwa kalikat ak'a piurtarkauyaaqellret
neq'aklukek elitnauristeqarraaput Iitaruaq Aangaarraaq-llu
taq'arput. Quyurmek allakarmek-llu angpartellruit amiiget
elitnaurvimteńi caliamegnegun unuaquaqan taqsuqengermek
elicesqumayaaqngamegneki elitnauraput Yugtun eliculriit.
Nangyuilngurmek waniwa ukuk quyavikagka umyuaqluki
ilanka elitnauristet Yugtun elitnauritulit nunacuarni.

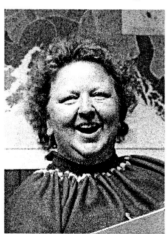 

Irene Iitaruaq Reed   Sophie Aangaarraaq Shield

Preface
Walkie Charles

In the fall of 1977, I was first introduced to Yup'ik as a second language when I was offered the privilege of teaching Yup'ik to elementary school students in my community of Emmonak. Being fresh out of boarding school, I found it ironic that I was asked to teach Yup'ik in the schools where a few years prior I had been one of those students who were forbidden to speak it.

My first reaction to this new assignment was, "How am I going to teach my language without any teaching experience?" I learned quickly that there were many Yup'ik people in a similar dilemma; they could speak both English and Yup'ik and had strong communication skills, but they needed training and materials for teaching. As instructor, I was offered the opportunity to participate in workshops in Yup'ik orthography, second-language teaching methods, games, and songs. Fortunately there were communities in other parts of the Yup'ik region where Yup'ik was still spoken by all ages. With the help of the Yup'ik Language Workshop, which had started at the University of Alaska Fairbanks (later moved to Bethel) to assist Yup'ik language teachers, I was on my way to acquiring the tools I needed to teach.

By 1977, the Yup'ik language program had published many traditional Yup'ik children's stories and original materials. It had also translated Euro-American stories such as *Cinderella (Caurluq)* and *Goldilocks and the Three Bears (Kul'tilakessa'aq Pingayun-llu Taqukat)* into Yup'ik, and these had proved to be very popular. Of all the materials I encountered as a new Yup'ik instructor, the children's songs that had been translated into Yup'ik were of greatest value. By the time I started to teach, there were several songbooks from which I was able to obtain music for my classroom.

Three people—Irene Iitaruaq Reed, Sophie Aangaarraaq Shield, and Esther Nuqaq'aq Green—were primarily responsible for bringing these children's favorites in song in the Yup'ik language to students in the bilingual program. I had the honor of learning from all three of these priceless teachers before, during, and after my tenure as Yup'ik instructor. The magic that Irene and Sophie had in chanting "Tang waniwa wiinga, nutaan itertua…" and "Kiarallruucircia wiinga…" immediately broke down barriers for me and gave me the confidence to teach my own language to my own people.

Irene, Sophie, and Esther empowered us, the Yup'ik classroom teachers, to transmit the magic of music into the hearts and souls of the youngsters we taught and continue to teach. It humbles me to enter classrooms in the Yup'ik region today and still hear the life of Irene and Sophie through the children who with passion, joy, and confidence sing the songs these teachers and their many associates created during the early days of Yup'ik programs in the 1970s.

This long-awaited songbook is dedicated in memory of our first teachers, Irene Iitaruaq Reed, and Sophie Aangaarraaq Shield. Together and separately, they opened the doors of the schools so that the Yup'ik language might flourish through the hours, months, and years of dedicated work to bring Yup'ik music into the ears of every child in Yup'ik Alaska.

Introduction

Steven A. Jacobson

In Kwethluk in the summer of 1973, I was quite surprised to hear children singing some of the Yup'ik songs that are presented in this songbook and on the accompanying CD. The lyrics had been composed for bilingual education programs that had started only two years before on a trial basis in four Lower Kuskokwim village schools. Kwethluk was not one of these schools, and it turned out that the children there had learned the songs from friends and relatives who lived upriver in Akiachak, which did have a bilingual program. In just two years, the songs had become part of Yup'ik children's culture, having been learned in school and then passed from person to person outside of school, just as the Yup'ik ditties or jingles that one says upon seeing a certain bug or bird are passed from child to child down through the years.

We cannot say exactly who composed the Yup'ik lyrics for each of these songs, but we know that Nuquq'aq, Esther Green, an elementary school teacher from Bethel, was responsible for quite a few, and Iitaruaq, Irene Reed, with her Yup'ik co-workers in Bethel and Fairbanks, came up with many others. Over time, a number of different school agencies published songbooks. Among these are *Yuarutet* (Eskimo Language Workshop, Fairbanks, 1972), *Aturpalta* (BIA Bilingual Education Center, Bethel, 1977), *Central Yupik: A Course in Spoken Eskimo* (Educational Research Associates, Albuquerque, 1977), *Nuqaq'am Yuarutai Elitnaurissuutet, Esther's Teaching Songs* (Yugtun Qaneryaramek Calivik, Bethel, 1979), and *Yup'ik Song Book* (Southwest Region Schools, Dillingham, 1982). The songs were recorded on tape, some of which were duplicated and distributed to bilingual teachers; one was formally produced (*Yupik Songs* to accompany *Central Yupik: A Course in Spoken Eskimo*).

Some of the songs are translations, exact or approximate, of familiar Euro-American children's songs; others use the melody of a well-known song but have a totally different content.

In 2001, when Irene Reed donated her extensive collection of papers and tape recordings to the Alaska Native Language Center, we were delighted to encounter the song recordings. Some of these were not of the best sound quality to start with, and some had deteriorated over time, but most could be restored to some extent. One can hear many familiar and beloved voices: Sophie Manutoli Shield, Irene Reed, Joseph Coolidge, Nellie Coolidge, Esther Green, Nastasia Nick

A page from *Yuarutet*, one of several song books published by school agencies in the 1970s. "Tanglaran-qaa Nasaurluyagaq?" is song 49 (p. 46) in the present book.

Hoffman and others. Sometimes the singers perform in groups with names such as "Yup'ik Bilingual Teachers' Chorus" and "Yugcetun Qaneryaramek Calivik Trio." Different singers have their own styles, as do different songwriters. For example, in the many songs composed and sung by Esther Green one can see how several syllables are compressed together to fit a single note and how one syllable is drawn out over several notes, just as in the tradition of Yup'ik hymn singing.

We have reproduced in this volume almost all the songs that remained in Irene Reed's collection. Sometimes we found two renditions of the same piece sung, for example, by a chorus one time and by a duet another time. In such cases, both are included. For one song, *Yaquleyagaq Atulria* (tracks 61-62), to our amazement, we found another version, titled *Süingassangaqatartua Nat'laangamek* (track 63), recorded on a reel-to-reel tape by Danish linguist Louis Hammerich perhaps as early as the 1950s. However, we could not determine either where Hammerich recorded the song or by whom it was sung. Possibly it came out of a Catholic boarding school on the Yukon and then was passed down for twenty years, in the school or outside, until adopted by the bilingual program.

Almost from the beginning of our work on this CD and songbook, we heard objections to the fact that, rather than tapping into a Native Yup'ik song tradition, these songs are Euro-American melodies with lyrics translated in many cases into Yup'ik from English. These objections, however, almost never came from Yup'ik people and certainly not from Yup'ik children, who love these songs.

Still, there is in fact an indigenous Yup'ik song tradition. In *Yup'ik Eskimo Songs* (Johnston and Pulu 1982a) and in *Koliganek Dance Songs* (Johnston and Pulu 1982b), one can find lyrics and music for shaman's songs, teasing songs, jump-rope songs, dance songs, teaching songs, and traveling songs from Toksook Bay, Kasigluk, and Pilot Station. Looking at these two books, one sees ancient songs as well as songs that have obviously modern references such as the alphabet and airplanes. There is also a continuing Yup'ik tradition of hymns and other Christian songs, many recorded and sold on LP records, cassette tapes, and CDs by Henry Shavings, Paul Jenkins, and others. One can see a link between the style of these church songs and some of the children's songs here.

Then there are the country and western songs adapted into Yup'ik by Joe Paul (LP record *Kuskokwim Song's and Story's* [*sic*]), the unique original Yup'ik songs of John Angaiak (LP record *I'm Lost in the City*, originally accompanied by a songbook, reissued as a CD by the Alaska Native Language Center) and of Chuna MacIntyre (cassette *Songs and Stories of the Yup'ik Eskimo*), songs by Peter Twitchell and Friends (the CD *Eskimo Jam*), and the innovative music of the group *Pamyua* (CD such as *Mengluni*), to name only a few. Yup'ik musical traditions and genres mix with each other, and the present collection should be viewed as one more ingredient in this mix.

The children's songs here are not the only ones made for the bilingual program over the years, but this collection probably includes a majority of them.

1
Erenret Atrit
(*On Sunday I Am Happy,*
On Monday Full Of Joy-m eriniikun)

Agayuneq, Pekyun, Aipirin, Pingayirin,
Cetamirin, Tallimirin, Maqineq-llu.
Agayuneq, Pekyun, Aipirin, Pingayirin,
Cetamirin, Tallimirin, Maqineq-llu.

2
Agluryaq
(*Down In The Valley*-m eriniikun)

Agluryaq alairqami ellami
Tangnirqerrlainatuuq kesianek.
Nallunairutnguuq wangkutnun
Ella assiilnguq
Quunengqata'arqan.

Utertaara
Qanuut, ellalluut, taituk, amirlut,
Ull'uyaq-llu ellamek tailartuq.

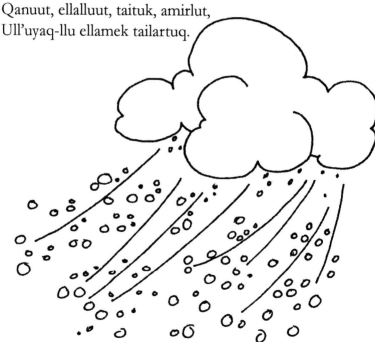

3
Alussistuaqegtaarmek Piamteggen
(*We Wish You A Merry Christmas*-am eriniikun)

Alussistuaqegtaarmek piamteggen,
Alussistuaqegtaarmek piamteggen,
Alussistuaqegtaarmek piamteggen,
Cali allrakuqegtaarmek.

(The Yup'ik is a translation of the song *We Wish You A Merry Christmas*.)

4
America
(*America The Beautiful*-am eriniikun)

America-q nunanirquq,
Tangniq'laami cakneq,
Ingrikayiit ucurnarqut
Nunarpiim qaingani.
America-q, *America*-q,
Naklekliu Agayutem.
Ilakiutevkarluki-llu
Yugugaat tamaita.

(The Yup'ik is a translation of the song *America The Beautiful*.)

5
Angniq Anutiiq
(*Happy Birthday*-m eriniikun)

Angniq anutiiq elpenun.
Angniq anutiiq elpenun.
Angniq anutiiq (yuum atra).
Angniq anutiiq elpenun.

(The Yup'ik is a translation of the song *Happy Birthday*.)

6
Arnam Atauciq Issuriq Ciumek Amiiraa
(*I've Been Working On The Railroad*-aam eriniikun)

Arnam atauciq issuriq ciumek amiiraa.
Aipaa unuaqu piciqaa taqsuqenrilkuni.
Kingumek-llu tau-i nutaan pingayuat piciqaa.
Nutaan-llu qaqiskuniki nillaqcaarluki.

7
Arnat Nem'eggni Caliuralartut
(*Home On The Range*-am eriniikun)

Arnat nem'eggni caliuralartut
Caliarkanek ernerpak.
Erenrem iquani taqsuqaarcameng,
Mernuinerciryupialartut.

Utertaara
Erenrem iquani,
Taqsuqngameng mernulartut.
Qavarluteng-llu inglerni uligluteng,
Putuskat pilialteng aturluki.

8-9
Avelngaat Pingayun
(Three Blind Mice-am eriniikun)

Avelngaat ukut
Pingayuuluteng
Aqvaqualriit
Cikmiumarmeng.
Malirqeraat arnaq kinguakun
Uluarluki pamyuit kep'artai.
Waten-qaa tangtuuci
Pilrianek avelngarnek?

(The Yup'ik is a translation of the song *Three Blind Mice*.)

10-11
Nervallalleq
(*Mary Had A Little Lamb*-am eriniikun)

Avelngacuar nerumalria
Amllernek, anllernek.
Tua-i-ll' aqsiqercami
Ellamun anluni.

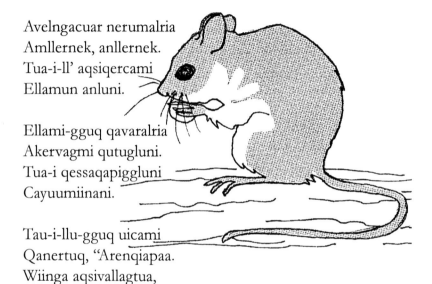

Ellami-gguq qavaralria
Akervagmi qutugluni.
Tua-i qessaqapiggluni
Cayuumiinani.

Tau-i-llu-gguq uicami
Qanertuq, "Arenqiapaa.
Wiinga aqsivallagtua,
Anllecillernek."

12
Ayagaciqukut
Nunakuarcuutetgun
(*The Farmer In The Dell*-am eriniikun)

Ayagaciqukut nunakuarcuutetgun
Akalrialuta ayagaciqukut.

Paissiikelarluta anglaniluta-llu
Tumyarat aturluki ayagaciqukut.

Ucitulirpagmun tamamta ekluta
Ayagaciqukut nunanun piciatun.

Velaspitarluta uciyaralagkun
Arulaiqsaunata ayagaciqukut.

Qanikcam qaingakun snuukuuraciqukut
Cukaunata cali-llu mulnguku'urluta.

Ellakun qulemteñi-llu tengssuutem iluani
Nunaarciiqukut yaaqvanun ayagluta.

13
Ayagalartukut
(*The Farmer In The Dell*-am eriniikun)

Ayagalartukut qayatgun mermi,
Anguarturluta mulngaku'urluta.

Ayagalartukut ellami tengssuutetgun,
Tengaurluta ellakun cukaqapiggluta.

Ayagalartukut nunakuarcuutetgun
Tumyaratgun kiingan pekqurluta.

Ayagalartukut uksumi qimugtetgun,
Ikamranek aturluta qanikcam qaingakun.

14
Calirpagtut Yuut
(*Silver Bells*-am eriniikun)

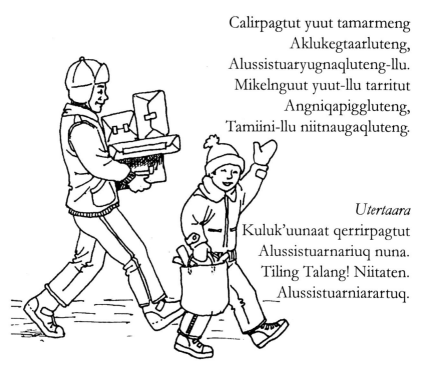

Calirpagtut yuut tamarmeng
Aklukegtaarluteng,
Alussistuaryugnaqluteng-llu.
Mikelnguut yuut-llu tarritut
Angniqapiggluteng,
Tamiini-llu niitnaugaqluteng.

Utertaara
Kuluk'uunaat qerrirpagtut
Alussistuarnariuq nuna.
Tiling Talang! Niitaten.
_Alussistuarniarartuq.

Tumyarani kenurrarluteng
Kavilriit cungaglit.
Tegutalirluteng utertut,
Niiski mikelnguut tamualriit.
Santam ernerpakaa
Niitaten-llu calirpalriit yuut.

15
Cav'urluten
(*Row Row Row Your Boat*-am eriniikun)

Cav'urluten-llu mulngaku'urluten
Angyami uvaaksaunak
Kanartaaqsaunak-llu.

16
Cetamauluteng Ukut Angyami

Cetamauluteng ukut angyami
Uitaluteng ulerpallrani.
Aqvalluteng kenegnalriamek,
Aqvalluteng kenegnalriamek.

Aqvaskina kenegnalriamek
Yuut qallatengraata canrituq.
Aqvallaut-llu kenegnalriamek,
Aqvallaut-llu kenegnalriamek.

Pingayuuluteng ukut angyami
Uqamailami uivesciiganani.
Aqvalluteng kenegnalriamek,
Aqvalluteng kenegnalriamek.

17
Minguut
(*Ten Little Indians*-am eriniikun)

Cungagliq, qiugliq, kavirliq, esirliq,
Tungulria, qatellria, perpelaaq, kavirrluk,
Nunapigngalnguq, palirta, marayarngalnguq,
Uurincaaq.

18
Ellallucuaraat Igqaqut
(*London Bridge*
Is Falling Down-am eriniikun)

Ellallucuaraat igqaqut, igqaqut, igqaqut.
Ellallucuaraat igqaqut, mecungnaqluteng.

Qanucuaraat igqaqut, igqaqut, igqaqut.
Qanucuaraat igqaqut, maqarceńateng.

Amirlucuaraat qilagmi, qilagmi, qilagmi.
Amirlucuaraat qilagmi, pugtaurluteng.

19
Ellamun Yuarun
(*Are You Sleeping*-am eriniikun)

Ellalluut igtut, ellalluut igtut
Unuamek, unuamek.
Mecungnaqeqapiarluteng, mecungnaqeqapiarluteng
Ellami qagaani.

Kavtuut igtut, kavtuut igtut
Caknerpak, caknerpak.
Kumlatqapiarluteng, kumlatqapiarluteng
Mikluteng, mikluteng.

Kallirtuq-am, kallirtuq-am,
Niitan-qaa, niitan-qaa?
Nutpaganganani, nutpaganganani
Qastupiaq, qastupiaq.

Anuqa taiguq, anuqa taiguq
Tuknilria, tuknilria.
Tengciiqaakut-llu-am, tengciiqaakut-llu-am
Yaaqvanun, yaaqvanun.

20
Ikayurtengqelartukut
(*Twinkle, Twinkle Little Star*-am eriniikun)

Ikayurtengqelartukut
Tangtukemteñek kesianek.
Nunamteñi elitnauristeñek.
Cali-llu iinriurteñek.
Ikayurtengqelartukut
Tangtukemteñek kesianek

Ikayurtengqelartukut
Ayuqevkenateng calituut
Ilait elitnauristeñguut
Ilait-llu iinriurteñguut
Tamarmeng yuut calilartut
Caliarit ayuqsuitut

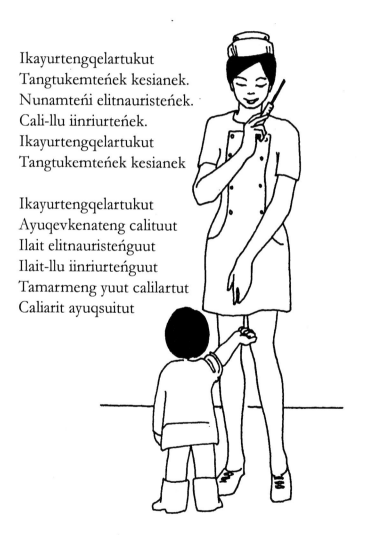

21
Kallaggluteng
(*Jingle Bells*-am eriniikun)

Kallaggluteng kuluk'uunaat
Kallagtut ayatmun
Anglanaqvaa ayanermi
Qimugciruarluni!

(The Yup'ik is an approximate translation of the English
song *Jingle Bells*.)

22
Kiarallgucircia Wiinga

Kiarallgucircia wiinga
Kiarallgucircia wiinga
Kitak tua-i qanrusnga.
Camek tangercit?
Tangrraqa, tangrraqa, tangrraqa (qangqiiq, angyaq, etc.).

23
Naaqutnun Yuarun
(*Baa, Baa, Black Sheep*-am eriniikun)

Kitak elpet naaqiqaa
Ataucimek ayagluten
Tekilluku-llu qula.
Kitak ampi ayagnia
Elitetassiarluten-llu
Taa-ta, taa-ta, taa-ta-ta.

1

2

Atauciq, malruk, pingayun,
Cetaman, talliman, arvinlegen,
Malrunlegen, pingayunlegen,
Qulngunrita'ar, qula-llu.
Tua-i wiinga elitanka
Nutaan-qaa, atam wiinga.

3

4 *5*

6

7 *8* *9*

24
Kuikaqa Man'a
(*Good Night, Ladies*-am eriniikun)

Kuikaqa man'a, kuikaqa man'a.
Kusquqvak man'a wiinga kuikaqa.

Kusquqvaak usuuq assikamken cakneq.
Kuikngamken nakmiin ceñavni yuurtellruama.

Neqkit'larpenga taryaqvagnek.
Qusuucuararnek kaigcessngaitarpenga.

25
Kuskaaq Nantellrusit?
(*Pussy Cat, Pussy Cat, Where Have You Been*-am eriniikun)

Kuskaaq, kuskaaq, nantellrusit?
Nunasngallruunga ellarpiim akiani.
Kuskaaq, kuskaaq, calillrusit?
Avelngaq alingallagcetellruaqa.

26-27
Maqaruaq Qeckalartuq
(*The Bear Went*
Over The Mountain-am eriniikun)

Maqaruaq qeckalartuq,
Maqaruaq qeckalartuq,
Maqaruaq qeckalartuq
Ayagaqami.
Pamyua mikluni,
Ciutek taklutek.
Maqaruaq qeckalartuq,
Maqaruaq qeckalartuq
Ayagaqami.

28
Mikelnguq Napami Uitalria
(*Rock-A-Bye, Baby*-m eriniikun)

Mikelnguq napami uitalria,
Anuqengkan anglaniciquq.
Napam avayaa asmeskan,
Mikelnguurluq-llu igciiquq.

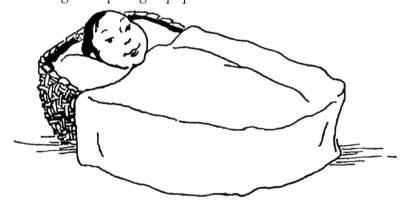

(The Yup'ik is a translation of the song *Rock-a-bye, Baby*.)

29
Natmun Qimugteka Tamarta?
(*Where Has My Little Dog Gone*-am eriniikun)

Natmun qimugteka tamarta?
Nani-kiq uitayarta?
Ciucecuarluni, pamyurpauluni
Nani-kiq uitayarta?

(The Yup'ik is a translation of the song *Where Has My Little Dog Gone?*)

30
Naucetaaqegtaaraat Arulauralriit
(*White Coral Bells*-am eriniikun)

Naucetaaqegtaaraat arulauralriit
Kuluk'uunatun elucingqerrluteng-llu
Tua-i niicugniyuuminritaten-qaa
Ircenrraat atu'urqata niitnaulartut.

(The Yup'ik is a translation of the song *White Coral Bells*.)

31
Nem Qainganun
(*Up On The Housetop*-am eriniikun)

Nem qainganun tuntut mit'ut,
Yuugartuq Santa Claus-aq.
Puyirvigkun naanguarutnek
Mikelnguut Alussistualarai.

Ho ho ho kina-kiq yuk
Ho ho ho piyuumiita?
Nem qaingalluni tem-tem-tem
Puyirvigkun tauna tuntulek.

Ciuqliqlukek nayagamun
Santa iminqegcaarluku.
Yuguaŭrluq ngel'atulria
Cikemqeqtaaraqluni-llu.

Ho ho ho kina-kiq yuk
Ho ho ho piyuumiita?
Nem qaingalluni tem-tem-tem
Puyirvigkun tauna tuntulek.

Aipaa-llu-kiq anngarpagmun
Tangrru imarturluni.
Mulut'uugmek ussukcanek
Angqaq piqrutarpak-wa.

(The Yup'ik is a translation of the song *Up On The Housetop*.)

32
Nunaka Elpet-llu
(*America*-m [*My Country 'Tis of Thee*-m] eriniikun)

Nunaka elpet-llu
Umyugiurvikarpuk
Atuutkamteggen.
Ciuliamta tuqullret
Pektaullret piyagutiit
(Caninermi) tamiini eriniateklaut!

(The Yup'ik is a translation of the song *America* [*My Country 'Tis of Thee*].)

33
Qamiqum (Nasqum) Ilai
(*Ten Little Indian Boys*-am eriniikun)

Nuyat, ciun, kegginaq, qauraq.
Qavluuk, iik, ulluvak, qengaq.
Qaneq, qerrluuk, keggutet, alungun.
Tamluq, uyaquq.

34
Qaariitaamun Yuarun

Qaariitaam unukuani kiima,
Tan'germi uterteqcaarallemni,
Alangrut kassugusngallruatnga,
Alingqapiarlua-llu wii puu-puu.

35
Qimugta Egalermi
(*How Much Is That Doggie In The Window*-m eriniikun)

Qaill' akingqerta qimugta egalermi? Au-au
Pekquratulimek pamyulek.
Qaill' akingqerta qimugta egalermi? Au-au
Tuniarusqumaaqa qimugta au-au.

(The Yup'ik is an approximate translation of the English
song *How Much Is That Doggie In The Window?*)

36
Qaillun Unuamek Ella Ayuqa?
(*Four In A Boat*-am eriniikun)

Qaillun unuamek ella ayuqa?
Qaillun unuamek ella ayuqa?
Qaillun unuamek ella ayuqa?
Qaillun unuamek ella ayuqa?

Unuamek ella akercirtuq.
Unuamek ella akercirtuq.
Unuamek ella akercirtuq.
Unuamek ella akercirtuq.

37
Erinairissuutmun Yuarun
(*Ten Little Indians*-am eriniikun)

Qalartellrianek wall' aturpagalrianek
Erinairilartukut erinairissuutetgun,
Caarkailkumta niicugniarkamteńek
Wall' elitnauqumta.

38
Qalarut'lartukut Igarataqamta
(*Farmer In The Dell*-am eriniikun)

Qalarut'lartukut igarataqamta
Piciatun yuullgutemteńun
Wall' kenkek'ngamteńun.

39
Temem Ilai
(*Are You Sleeping*-am eriniikun)

Qamiquq, tusgek, ciisquk, it'gak.
Elitanka, elitanka.
Qamiquq, tusgek, ciisquk.
It'gak, qamiquq, tusgek
Ciisquk, it'gak.

40
Qanuut Igtut
(*Are You Sleeping*-am eriniikun)

Qanuut igtut, qanuut igtut ernerpak, ernerpak.
Tangniqvagtat cakneq, tangniqvagtat cakneq.
Tangerki, tangerki.

41
Qavanguqa Alussistuaq
(*White Christmas*-am eriniikun)

Qavanguqa Alussistuaq
Nallunrit'lallemtun-llu wii
Napat qaingit qerrirpak
Mikelnguut niitaat ikamraq qanikcarmi.

Qavanguqa Alussistuaq
Umyuaqutet igallrenka
Erneten tanqigikilit
Alussistuaqegcikina-llu.

(The Yup'ik is an approximate translation of the English
song *White Christmas*.)

42
Qavartuten-qaa?
(*Are You Sleeping*-am eriniikun)

Qavartuten-qaa, qavartuten-qaa,
Anngaurluuq, anngaurluuq?
Kuluk'uunaq kaugtuq, kuluk'uunaq kaugtuq.
Tiling talang tiling. Tiling talang tiling.

(The Yup'ik is an approximate translation of the English
song *Are You Sleeping?*)

43-44
Quyaunga Uqsuqayaaruama
(*The Little White Duck*-am eriniikun)

Quyaunga uqsuqayaaruama, quyaunga uqsuqayaaruama.
Kayangumek/Peksumek anellruunga, anglirikuma
   tengaurciqua.
Quyanaqvaa uqsuqaullinilua, ayuqaitua.

Quyaunga Yupiaruama wiinga, quyaunga Yupiaruama
   wiinga.
Aanamnek anellruunga, anglirikuma elisngariciqua.
Quyanaqvaa Yupiarullinilua, ayuqaitua.

45
Suulutaat Agyat
(*Alaska's Flag*-am eriniikun)

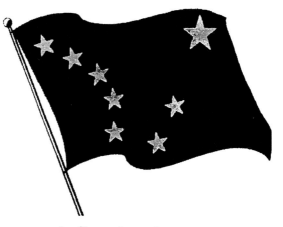

Suulutaat agyat qiuglim qaingani
Alaskam pelii elpenun piuli.
Qiuglia imarpiim atakuyartua ellam
Ingrit nanvait nunam naunrai-llu.
Yuungnaqellriit piyupialarait
Nunam tukuutai kuiget-llu.
Tanqigpalriit agyat uksumi,
Taqukaq, Qaluurin, tanqigpalriit.
Agyarrliim qulvani kenurralaraa
Ciqinqalaraa-llu ellarpiim qainga.
Alaskaam pelii, Alaskaqegtaarmun
Pelakegtaaraput tamalkumta.

46
Tan'gerlim Kiartellra
(*The Bear Went Over The Mountain*-am eriniikun)

Tan'gerliq ingrikun tev'uq. Tan'gerliq ingrikun tev'uq.
Tan'gerliq ingrikun tev'uq paqnayuqapiggluni.
Paqnayuqapiggluni, paqnayuqapiggluni.
Ingrim akmatiinek, ingrim akmatiinek
Ingrim akmatiinek kiingan tangerrnaqaa.

(The Yup'ik is an approximate translation of the English
song *The Bear Went Over The Mountain*.)

47
Tang, Waniwa Wiinga
(*In The Good Old Summertime*-am eriniikun)

Tang, waniwa wiinga
Nutaan itertua.
Wani aqumgaciqua
Qaqiutnatkamnun.
Igarcuun-llu wantuq
Yuarumalalqa,
Nutaan nangerteksaunii
Caliqcaarciqua.

48
Tangeqsaitan-qaa Qimugta
(*Did You Ever See A Lassie*-m eriniikun)

Tangeqsaitan-qaa qimugta, qimugta, qimugta?
Tangeqsaitan-qaa qimugta maaggun wall' avaggun?
Maaggun wall' avaggun, maaggun wall' avaggun?
Tangeqsaitan-qaa qimugta maaggun wall' avaggun?

49
Tanglaran-qaa Nasaurluyagaq?
(*Did You Ever See A Lassie*-m eriniikun)

Tanglaran-qaa nasaurluyagaq, nasaurluyagaq?
Tanglaran-qaa nasaurluyagaq waten pilria:
Ayalria ukatmun, tamaatmun, avatmun?
Tanglaran-qaa nasaurluyagaq waten pilria?

Tanglaran-qaa tan'gaurluyagaq, tan'gaurluyagaq?
Tanglaran-qaa tan'gaurluyagaq waten pilria:
Ayalria ukatmun, tamaatmun, avatmun?
Tanglaran-qaa tan'gaurluyagaq waten pilria?

50-51
Tanqiktaalria Agyacuar
(*Twinkle, Twinkle Little Star*-am eriniikun)

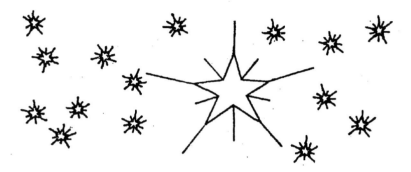

Tanqiktaalria agyacuar
Caucin paqnak'larqa wii.
Ak'akii ellam quliini
Qilkirtaatun qilagmi.
Tanqiktaalria agyacuar
Caucin paqnak'larqa wii.

(The Yup'ik is an approximate translation of the English
song *Twinkle, Twinkle Little Star*.)

52
Uksumi Kuigkun Manaryalartukut
(*She'll Be Coming Round The Mountain*-am eriniikun)

Uksumi kuigkun manaryalartukut
Cikum qaingakun anlualirraarluta.
Caaqamta iliini amllernek neqnek cangliqaqluta.
Uksumi kuigkun manaryalartukut.

53
Unuamek Elitukut Naaqiyaramek
(*Down By The Station*-am eriniikun)

Unuamek elitukut naaqiyaramek.
Naaqut'liuryaramek igaryaramek-llu.
Waten sass'aq ellian uterrnarituuq.

54
Unuamek Elitukut, Elitukut
(*Mary Had A Little Lamb*-am eriniikun)

Unuamek elitukut, elitukut, elitukut.
Unuamek elitukut amllernek canek.

Waniwa uterrnariuq, uterrnariuq, uterrnariuq.
Waniwa uterrnariuq; tua-i-ngunrituq.

55
Unukuani Sass'am
(*Hickory Dickory Dock*-am erinii)

Unukuani sass'am
Avelngaq mayurtuq.
Sass'aq kaugtuq
Ataucirqumek,
Avelngaq atraqertuq.

(The Yup'ik is a translation of the English song *Hickory Dickory Dock*.)

56
Waniwa Kuluvaaq

Waniwa kuluvaaq qaillun neplitua? Muu, muu.
Waniwa qimugta qaillun neplitua? Wuuvv, wuuvv.
Waniwa kuuskaaq qaillun neplitua? Mi-au, mi-au.
Waniwa cetayaaq qaillun neplitua? Cet-Cet.

57
Waniwa Uterrnariuq
(*The Mulberry Bush*-am eriniikun)

Waniwa uterrnariuq, uterrnariuq, uterrnariuq.
Waniwa uterrnariuq, unuaqu, tainiartuci.

58
Qalarucaraq
(*White Coral Bells*-am eriniikun)

Waqaa cangacit? Assirtua kituusit?
Waqaa cangacit? Assirtua kituusit?
Waqaa cangacit? Assirtua kituusit?
Waqaa cangacit? Assirtua kituusit?

59
Waten Aquilartukut
(*The Mulberry Bush*-am eriniikun)

Waten aquilartukut –lartukut –lartukut.
Waten aquilartukut unuakuayaarmi.

Waten qacarqaulartukut –lartukut –lartukut.
Waten qacarqaulartukut unuakuayaarmi.

Waten uvaalartukut –lartukut –lartukut.
Waten uvaalartuku unuakuayaarmi.

Waten cav'uralartukut –lartukut –lartukut.
Waten cav'uralartukut unuakuayaarmi.

Waten angualartukut –lartukut –lartukut.
Waten angualartukut unuakuayaarmi.

Waten yuralartukut –lartukut –lartukut.
Waten yuralartukut unuakuayaarmi.

Waten tengaulartukut –lartukut –lartukut.
Waten tengaulartukut unuakuayaarmi.

60
Waten Erurilartukut
(*Little Darling I Love You*-m eriniikun)

Waten erurilartukut unateput iqaaqata.
Waten ermilartukut kegginaput iqangaqan.
Waten iqairilartukut akluput iqaaqata.
Waten erurilartukut saskaput uqlarqata.
Waten suugilartukut naterput iqangaqan.
Waten kagilartukut nateq caarrlingaqan.

61-62
Yaquleyagaq Atulria
(*Buffalo Gals*-am eriniikun)

Yaquleyagaq-gguq napam qaingani, napam qaingani,
Napam qaingani.
Yaquleyagaq-gguq napam qaingani
Aturpagtuq wangnun.

63
Siingassangaqatartuq
Nat'laangamek

Siingassangaqatartua, saangaqatartua nat'laangamek.

Yaquleyagar napani napani napani,
Yaquleyagar napani aturluni pilria.

Yaquleyagar napani napani napani,
Yaquleyagar napani aturluni pilria.

Yaquleyagar napani napani napani,
Yaquleyagar napani aturluni pilria.

64
Yuilquq Kiagmi Egturyalipiartuq
(*On Top Of Old Smokey*-m eriniikun)

Yuilquq kiagmi egturyalipiartuq.
Eqnaripialartut keggmangaqameng.

Taũgaam keneq ekualria assikenritaat,
Aruvilaan cakneq ekuagaqami.

65
Yuut Uitalriit Ellamteńi

Yuut uitalriit ellamteńi
Ilangqetuut tamarmeng.
Aanat aatat-llu cali
Angayuqauluteng.

English Titles and Translations

1
Sunday Monday
(To the tune of *On Sunday I Am Happy, On Monday Full Of Joy*)

Sunday, Monday, Tuesday, Wednesday,
Thursday, Friday, and Saturday.
Sunday, Monday, Tuesday, Wednesday,
Thursday, Friday, and Saturday.

2
The Rainbow
(To the tune of *Down In The Valley*)

When the rainbow appears in the air
It always looks pretty.
It is a sign to us
The weather that's bad
Is going to calm down.

Chorus
Snowflakes, raindrops, fog, clouds,
And the whirlwind comes from the air.

3
We Wish You A Merry Christmas

(The Yup'ik is a translation of the song *We Wish You A Merry Christmas*.)

4
America The Beautiful

(The Yup'ik is an approximate translation of the song *America The Beautiful*.)

5
Happy Birthday

(The Yup'ik is a translation of the song *Happy Birthday*.)

6
The Woman Skins One Seal First
(To the tune of *I've Been Working on the Railroad*)

The woman skins one seal first.
She'll skin the second one tomorrow if she is not tired.
And then last of all she will skin the third one.
Then when she is finished with them she will stretch them
out to dry.

7
Women Work In Their Houses Continuously
(To the tune of *Home on the Range*)

Women work in their houses continuously,
Things to do all day.
At the end of the day when they are tired,
They want to rest very much.

Chorus
At the end of the day,
When they are tired, they are exhausted.
They sleep on the bed with blankets,
Using the pillows that they made.

8-9
Three Blind Mice

(The Yup'ik is a translation of the song *Three Blind Mice*.)

10-11
The Overeater
(To the tune of *Mary Had A Little Lamb*)

The little mouse keeps eating
Tall cottongrass tubers, tall cottongrass tubers.
Then when he is full up
Outside he goes.

Sleeping outside,
Snoring in the sunlight,
Feeling lethargic,
Not wanting to do anything.

And so when he opens his eyes,
He says, "Oh dear
I'm so full
Of these tall cottongrass tubers."

12
We Will Travel With Cars
(To the tune of *The Farmer in the Dell*)

We will travel with cars
Rolling along we will travel.

Going by bicycle we will have a good time too
Following the road we will travel.

We will all get into the big load carrier
We will travel to any lands.

We will go by velocipede with ones that can carry loads
Without stopping we will travel.

On the surface of the snow we will go by snowmachine
Slowly and carefully.

Through the air above us inside an airplane
We will visit far away traveling.

13
We Travel
(To the tune of *The Farmer in the Dell*)

We travel with kayaks on the water
Paddling and being very careful.

We travel in the air with airplanes.
Flying in the air very fast.

We travel with cars
On the road only we move along.

We travel in winter with dogteams,
We use sleds in the snow.

14
People Work Hard
(To the tune of *Silver Bells*)

All people are working hard
Putting on good clothes,
Preparing for Christmas.
Children and adults walk around
Having lots of fun.
Everywhere one can hear them.

Chorus
Bells sparkle
It's time for Christmas in the land.
Ding dong, you hear them,
They will soon celebrate Christmas.

There are lights on the roads
Red and green.
They return home with gifts,
Hear the children chewing treats.
It's Santa's big day,
And you hear the hard-working people.

15
Keep Rowing
(To the tune of *Row Row Row Your Boat*)

Keep rowing carefully
In the boat without rocking
And avoid leaning too far toward the water.

16
These Four In a Boat

These four in a boat
Being there when there is a flood.
Fetching a pretty one,
Fetching a pretty one.

Fetch a pretty one
It's OK even if people talk.
Let's fetch a pretty one,
Let's fetch a pretty one.

These three in a boat
Because it's heavy it can't turn.
Fetching a pretty one,
Fetching a pretty one.

17
Colors
(To the tune of *Ten Little Indians*)

Green, blue, red, yellow
Black, white, purple, pink,
Brown, tan, gray,
Orange.

18
Little Raindrops Keep Falling
(To the tune of *London Bridge is Falling Down*)

Little raindrops keep falling, keep falling, keep falling.
Little raindrops keep falling, getting one wet.

Little snowflakes keep falling, keep falling, keep falling.
Little snowflakes keep falling, being soft and warm.

Little clouds in the sky, in the sky, in the sky.
Little clouds in the sky keep coming to the surface.

19
Song to the Weather
(To the tune of *Are You Sleeping*)

Raindrops are falling, raindrops are falling,
Today, today.
Very wet, very wet
In the air out there.

Hail stones are falling, hail stones are falling,
Very hard, very hard.
Very cold, very cold
Being small, being small.

There is thunder, there is thunder,
Do you hear it? Do you hear it?
With a bang, with a bang
Very loud, very loud.

Wind is coming, wind is coming,
Strong, strong.
It will blow us away, it will blow us away
To a distant place, to a distant place.

20
We Have Helpers
(To the tune of *Twinkle, Twinkle Little Star*)

We have helpers
The ones we see all the time
At our villages, teachers
And health aides too.
We have helpers.
The ones we see all the time.

We have helpers.
Each has a different job.
Some of them are teachers.
And some of them are nurses.
All people work.
Their jobs are not alike.

21
Jingle Bells

(The Yup'ik is a translation of the English song *Jingle Bells*.)

22
Look Around the Room With Me

Look around the room with me
Look around the room with me
Tell me what you see.
I see, I see, I see a (ptarmigan, boat, etc.).

23
Song to the Numbers
(To the tune of *Baa, Baa, Black Sheep*)

Hurry up and count
Beginning from one
All the way to ten.
Hurry and begin
And see how much you have learned.
Taa-ta, taa-ta, taa-ta-ta.

One, two, three,
Four, five, six,
Seven, eight,
Nine, and ten.
Now I've learned
How good I am now.

24
This Is My River
(To the tune of *Good Night, Ladies*)

This is my river, this is my river.
The Kuskokwim is my river.

Kuskokwim, I like you very much.
You are my own because I was born on your shores.

You provide me with king salmon.
You've never deprived me of smelt.

25
Cat, Cat, Where Are You?
(To the tune of *Pussy Cat, Pussy Cat, Where Have You Been?*)

Cat, cat, where are you?
I was visiting on the other side of the world.
Cat, cat, what were you doing?
I frightened a mouse.

26-27
The Rabbit Hops
(To the tune of *The Bear Went Over The Mountain*)

The rabbit hops,
The rabbit hops,
The rabbit hops
When it travels.
With a short tail
And long ears,
The rabbit hops,
The rabbit hops
When it travels

28
Rock-a-bye, Baby

(The Yup'ik is a translation of the song *Rock-a-bye, Baby.*)

29
Where Has My Little Dog Gone?

(The Yup'ik is a translation of the song *Where Has My Little Dog Gone?*)

30
White Coral Bells

(The Yup'ik is a translation of the song *White Coral Bells*.)

31
Up On The Housetop

(The Yup'ik is a translation of the song *Up On The Housetop*.)

32
America (My Country 'Tis of Thee)

(The Yup'ik is a translation of the song *America* [*My Country 'Tis of Thee*].)

33
The Parts of the Head
(To the tune of *Ten Little Indian Boys*)

Hair, ear, face, forehead.
Eyebrows, eyes, cheek, nose.
Mouth, lips, teeth, tongue.
Chin, neck.

34
Song For Halloween

On Halloween night while alone,
In the dark as I was going home,
The ghosts were all around me,
And I was very scared, boo-boo.

35
How Much Is That Doggie In The Window?

(The Yup'ik is a translation of the song *How Much Is That Doggie In The Window?*)

36
How Is The Weather Today?
(To the tune of *Four In A Boat*)

How is the weather today?
How is the weather today?
How is the weather today?
How is the weather today?

The weather is sunny.
The weather is sunny.
The weather is sunny.
The weather is sunny.

37
Tape Recorder Song
(To the tune of *Ten Little Indians*)

People who are talking or singing
We record them with a tape recorder,
So that we can listen to them when we have no chores
Or when we are in school.

38
We Speak to Each Other When We Write Letters
(To the tune of *The Farmer in the Dell*)

We speak to each other when we write letters
To any other people
Or to our loved ones.

39
Parts of the Body
(To the tune of *Are You Sleeping?*)

Head, shoulders, knees, and feet.
I'm learning them, and learning them.
Head, shoulders, knees, and feet.
Feet, head, shoulders
Knees, and feet.

40
Snowflakes Are Falling
(To the tune of *Are You Sleeping?*)

Snowflakes are falling, snowflakes are falling today, today.
How beautiful, how beautiful.
Look at them, look at them.

41
White Christmas

(The Yup'ik is a translation of the song *White Christmas.*)

42
Are You Sleeping?

(The Yup'ik is a translation of the song *Are You Sleeping?*)

43-44
I'm Glad I'm a Little Duck
(To the tune of *Little White Duck*)

I'm glad I'm a little duck, I'm glad I'm a little duck.
I came out of an egg, when I grow up I will fly.
I'm grateful to be a little duck, I'm one of a kind.

I'm glad to be Yup'ik, I'm glad to be Yup'ik.
I came from my mother, when I grow up I will be
knowledgeable.
I'm grateful to be Yup'ik, I'm one of a kind.

45
Alaska's Flag

Golden Stars
Gold stars on a surface of blue
Alaska's flag let it be to you
The blue of the sea, the evening sky
The mountains, lakes, and the land's plants.
Those striving to live do really use
The riches of the land and rivers.
The bright stars in the winter
The Bear, the Dipper, the brilliant ones.
Polaris above all shining on it
Letting its rays flow out over the surface of the earth.
Alaska's flag to wonderful Alaska
Our great flag, all of us.

46
The Bear Went Over The Mountain

(The Yup'ik is a translation of the song *The Bear Went Over The Mountain*.)

47
Look, Here I Am
(To the tune of *In The Good Old Summertime*)

Look, here I am.
I just came in now.
I'll be sitting here
Until I am finished.
The pencil is right here too,
The one I searched for for so long.
Now without getting up
I will continue working.

48
Did You Ever See A Lassie?

Have you ever seen a dog, a dog, a dog?
Have you ever seen a dog going this way or that?
This way or that way, this way or that way?
Have you ever seen a dog going this way or that?

49
Do You See A Little Girl?
(To the tune of *Did You Ever See A Lassie?*)

Do you see a little girl, a little girl, a little girl?
Do you see a little girl doing this:
Coming this way, that way, away.
Do you see a little girl doing this?

Do you see a little boy, a little boy, a little boy?
Do you see a little boy doing this:
Coming this way, that way, away.
Do you see a little boy doing this?

50-51
Twinkle, Twinkle Little Star

(The Yup'ik is a translation of the song *Twinkle, Twinkle Little Star*.)

52
In The Winter We Go Ice Fishing On The River
(To the tune of *She'll Be Coming Round The Mountain*)

In the winter we go ice fishing on the river
On top of the ice after making a hole.
Sometimes we catch a lot of fish.
In the winter we go ice fishing on the river.

53
Today We Are Learning
(To the tune of *Down By The Station*)

Today we are learning how to count,
How to count and how to write.
When it's time we will go home.

54
Today We Are Learning
(To the tune of *Mary Had A Little Lamb*)

We are learning today, today, today.
We are learning a lot today.

It is time to go home, to go home, to go home.
It is is time to go home; so long.

55
Hickory Dickory Dock

(The Yup'ik is a translation of the song *Hickory Dickory Dock*.)

56
Here Is a Cow

Here is a cow. What sound does in make? Moo, moo.
Here is a dog. What sound does it make? Woof, woof.
Here is a cat. What sound does it make? Meow, meow.
Here is a little bird. What sound does it make? Chirp, chirp.

57
It Is Time To Go Home
(To the tune of *The Mulberry Bush*)

It is time to go home, to go home, to go home.
It is time to go home, so you'll come back tomorrow.

58
Hello, How Are You?
(To the tune of *White Coral Bells*)

Hello, how are you? I'm fine, who are you?
Hello, how are you? I'm fine, who are you?
Hello, how are you? I'm fine, who are you?
Hello, how are you? I'm fine, who are you?

59
This Is How We Play Outside
(To the tune of *The Mulberry Bush*)

This is how we play outside, play outside, play outside.
This is how we play outside early in the morning.

This is how we clap our hands, clap our hands, clap our hands.
This is how we clap our hands early in the morning.

This is how we rock the boat, rock the boat, rock the boat.
This is how we rock the boat early in the morning.

This is how we row the boat, row the boat, row the boat.
This is how we row the boat early in the morning.

This is how we paddle, paddle, paddle.
This is how we paddle early in the morning.

This is how we dance, dance, dance.
This is how we dance early in the morning.

This is how we fly, fly, fly.
This is how we fly early in the morning.

60
This Is The Way We Wash
(To the tune of *Little Darling I Love You*)

This is the way we wash when our hands get dirty.
This is the way we wash when our face gets dirty.
This is the way we wash when our clothes get dirty.
This is the way we wash when our dishes get dirty.
This is the way we wash when our floor gets dirty.
This is the way we sweep when the floor gets dirty.

61-62
Little Birdie Singing
(To the tune of *Buffalo Gals*)

Little birdie on the treetop, on the treetop,
On the treetop.
Little birdie on the treetop
Is singing loudly to me.

63
I'm Going To Sing A Song, Not A Long One

This rendition of "Yaquleyagaq Atulria" is from a tape recording, probably made on the Yukon, by the Danish linguist Hammerich perhaps as early as the 1950s.

64
Wilderness In The Summer Has Many Mosquitoes
(To the tune of *On Top Of Old Smokey*)

Wilderness has many mosquitoes in the summer.
They are very bothersome when they begin to bite.

But they don't like the fire burning,
Because the fire smokes a lot when it's burning.

65
People In Our World

People in our world
All of them have families.
Mothers and fathers too
Are parents.

References

Books

Bureau of Indian Affairs. Bilingual Education Center. 1977. *Aturpalta*. Bethel, Alaska: Oregon College of Education.

Eskimo Language Workshop. 1972. *Yuarutet*. Fairbanks: Department of Linguistics and Foreign Languages, University of Alaska.

Green, Esther. 1979. *Nuqaq'am Yuarutai Elitnaurissuutet (Esther's Teaching Songs)*. Bethel: Taqellret Yugtun Qaneryaramek Calivigmi, Kuskokwim Community College.

Johnston, Thomas F. and Tupou L. Pulu. 1982a. *Yup'ik Eskimo Songs*. Anchorage: Materials Development Center Rural Education University of Alaska.

Johnston, Thomas F. and Tupou L. Pulu. 1982b. *Koliganek Dance Songs*. Anchorage: Bilingual Education Program of the Southwest Region School District, and Materials Development Center Rural Education University of Alaska.

Southwest Region Schools. 1979. *Yup'ik Song Book*. Dillingham.

Tennant, Edward A. and Robert J. Rebert. 1977. *Central Yupik: A Course in Spoken Eskimo*. Albuquerque, N.M.: Educational Research Associates.

Sound Recordings

This is not a complete listing of recorded Yup'ik music. These items are merely representative of the depth and variety of artists and recordings in the field.

Angaiak, John. *I'm Lost in the City* (LP record). Fairbanks: Eskimo Language Workshop. (Re-issued on CD by the Alaska Native Language Center, Fairbanks.)

Green, Esther and Molly Lomack. *Yup'ik Songs* (cassette tape) to accompany *Central Yupik: A Course in Spoken Eskimo*. Albuquerque, N.M.: Educational Research Associates.

Jenkins, Paul. Paul Jenkins and Family. *I'll Rise to Shine* (cassette tape).

MacIntyre, Chuna. *Songs and Stories of the Yup'ik Eskimo* (cassette tape). Wild Sanctuary Music and Word Series WSC 1603.

Pamyua. *Mengluni* (CD). Ellavut Records 1109801.

Paul, Joe. *Country & Western Favorites* (LP record). Angelus Records WR 4997.

Paul, Joe. *Kuskokwim Song's and Story's* (sic) (LP record). Angelus Records WR 4940.

Paul, Joe. *Songs of Inspiration* (LP record). Angelus Records WR 4873.

Shavings, Henry. Henry Shavings and His Trio. *Home by the Bering Sea*. Angleus Records WR 4972.

Shavings, Henry and Hilma. *Redeemed* (CD). Gospel Music Ministries.

Twitchell, Peter. Peter Twitchell & Friends. *Eskimo Jam* (CD). Turnaround Productions TPCA01.

Index of Yup'ik Titles

Index of English Titles